LEGAL SUPPORT WORKER

CAREER

Careers Collection

By

Anne Johnson

Digital Edition V 1.0

Copyright 2016 by Careers Collection

Careers Collection

Contents

INTRODUCTION

I'll keep it short and sweet. This book will give you very good overview of what you will need to get your dream job and get promoted.

There are different ways of reading these types of books but here is the best way to read this one.

Quickly skim through it and look through the chapters. If an idea grabs you go with it and dig deeper down that rabbit hole.

You want to keep being excited as this will be a long road.

Once you're done then get back to the beginning.

Read through the book quickly.

Read again and take notes.

CAREER BACKGROUND

Each role in an organization or business is important and has its main functions. Usually, the higher positions don't have time to take care of the clerical duties of their department. For instance, lawyers also need support regarding paper works and clerical duties. The ones who provide this are called legal workers.

Legal support workers basically provide support mainly administrative and clerical duties for lawyers. There are over 45,570 legal workers in the United States. There is a 2% increase in employment over the past couple of years.

EXPECTED SALARY

The salary of legal support workers depends on various factors such as experience, employment status, and job setting.

The starting salary of a legal support worker is usually around $24,746 per year; the average salary is $41,192 per year. The highest salary a legal support worker makes is up to $48,466 annually.

DUTIES & RESPONSIBILITIES

The legal support workers are involved in different duties and responsibilities that should be accomplished on a regular basis. Their main responsibility is to provide support to lawyers, mainly taking care of all the clerical or administrative duties or activities.

This career is also involved in tasks such as accomplishing all organization goals and plans, conducting and analyzing legal articles and researches, doing administrative duties such as preparing documents and appeals, maintaining records, writing reports, ordering of supplies, organizing cases, coordinating with clients, performing lawyer requests, preparing budgets, taking phone calls, making phone calls, keeping records, filing and sorting.

EDUCATION REQUIRED

The legal support worker profession requires a college degree, which can be obtained in different colleges and universities. You should also further your studies and training by obtaining certification from seminars and other classes.

This career requires a license and should become a certified legal worker, but it depends on the state you are in and where you will choose to practice.

PERSONALITY

Legal support workers are responsible for performing support for lawyers such as clerical and administrative duties.

Aside from the knowledge and skill this career requires, legal support workers must be incredibly patient because they will be working long hours. They must be incredibly organized and have a good sense of judgment. They must be able to communicate well with people. It is also very important that they are professional at all times.

CAREER ETHICS (Do's and Don'ts)

Once you find a job, it is your responsibility to know the proper etiquette or the things you should do and shouldn't do at work. It is important to exude a positive persona that will not only boost morale, but will also help you build a good relationship with your colleagues and boss and that benefits you more than anyone else.

DO'S

Go to work on time. Time is of the essence, and professionalism will bring you to great heights.

As an employee, you need be respectful to your superior or boss at all times. There will be instances or situations that he/she will test your patience, but remember that your attitude at work is observed. Just because you are good at your job, it doesn't mean that you're indispensable.

Maintain a friendly attitude around your colleagues. Having a good relationship with your colleagues will make your life easier especially during a very stressful workday.

Dress appropriately. It is important to look presentable every single day at work because it will boost your self-confidence and add personality when you know you look good. Plus, you represent the company you work for.

You must know the workplace jargon. Avoid using offensive words and profanity because it will affect your performance. Learn how to express yourself respectfully and clearly in verbal and written form.

Do listen and be open-minded to constructive criticisms because it will help you improve your work. Be willing to learn new skills.

Follow the rules and regulations to avoid getting in trouble; Work with integrity and dedication.

DON'TS

Do not be afraid to ask. If you don't understand something, ask help from other people. It is better to ask first before you do something, than work on it right away and just make too much mistakes.

Avoid complaining. Complaining is a negative attitude that not only affects your image, but your job as well. If you're in a bad mood, it will definitely show in the quality of your work. Bad attitude could be a cause for your dismissal.

Do not engage in office gossips or banter because it will not only affect the other party involved, but your reputation as well. Focus on improving your skills rather than meddling in other people's business.

Do not invade your colleagues' personal space. It is important to keep a distance, but not too distant because it will give them a bad impression.

Don't be late for work. Let your superiors know if you can't make it on time if let's say, you have to do something very important. The same goes if you need to stay home. Not letting your boss know where you are or not being able to provide plausible reasons for your lateness could cost you your job.

Avoid posting on your social media while at work. You need to keep things professional. It is also important to avoid using your cellphone at your workplace.

LANDING A JOB INTERVIEW

Now, before you get a job, of course you will need to find an employer. And in order to do that, you must land a job interview. This chapter is all about teaching you the importance of a resume and cover letter in landing the job of dreams.

A resume can quickly tell an employer the important things they need to learn about a job candidate. Like what they say, first impressions last. So a good resume is vital especially in a very competitive industry. A resume has all the necessary information an employer would need to know first about a job applicant. It has details such as the candidate's name, the candidate's contact details, the name of the school he/she went to, where he/she had his/her internship, the number of jobs the candidate had and the companies they worked for, the achievements attained, and the skills the candidate has and acquired throughout the years. Your resume should attract attention first and foremost. You must remember that you are fighting with, well, probably a hundred other job candidates for that one coveted job.

Job resumes can be done in a couple of different formats. There's the chronological format and the functional format. Candidates who are looking for a job and at the same time, hoping to stay in the same field mostly use chronological formats. It is also suited for those candidates with a stable work history and if job requirements match your past job titles. Fresh graduates, as well as those who are looking into a career change use functional resumes. Those with a variety of skills and work experiences, whether related or not also use this format. Regardless of the resume you use, you need to understand that employers look for the same thing.

Now, a good resume can definitely help you land a job interview, but you must also know that a bad cover letter can also hurt your chances of getting a chance to sell yourself to an employer. Cover letters are extremely important in landing a job interview because it shows a candidate's work ethic as well as their keen attention to detail. Cover letters provide a foretaste of a candidate's personality, something most resumes cannot do.

Yes, resumes give the employers an impression of how good you are as an employee or a student, but cover letters provide them something else such as how well you follow instructions. It also tells an employer whether you can communicate well or how your skills and knowledge about the job are relevant. A good cover letter also separates you from your competitors with let's say, more achievements and work experiences. Most employers choose to have a dedicated and passionate individual than someone with an achiever who doesn't even have those, so it is very important to show your personality when working on your cover letter and show them a glimpse of who you are as an individual and what you would be like to have as an employee.

WAYS TO SELL YOURSELF EFFECTIVELY

So once you are scheduled to come in for a job interview, the next thing you need to think about is how to sell yourself. Selling yourself is the same thing as marketing yourself. Your future employer needs to know exactly why he or she should choose you from a pool of job candidates. This chapter will help you get an idea of the different conversational skills, as well as the different personality traits an employer looks for a job candidate.

One of the ways you can effectively sell yourself is to know the company. It is important develop the correct mindset when you come in for a job interview, and in order to do this, you must know your future employer. Familiarize yourself with the company, its products, its mission and vision and the traits employees have that contributed to the success of the company. You should be able to know what the company is all about and how your skills will help the company's growth.

Confidence is key. When you know yourself and the skills vital to the role you're a willing to play, the employer will see it. Employers want any job candidate to give them reasons why they're the perfect person for the job. Highlight the skills you have that will make you stand out from the rest of applicants. However, it is also wrong to overdo your confidence. Avoid talking about yourself too much; limit it to a minute. Be yourself and show your true personality while still using professional speech.

Another way of selling yourself is to relate some of your personal experiences to some of the skills the job is requiring. For instance, let the employer know about how you handled a specific event in your life or a situation you encountered during your time with a different company. Talk about the things you managed to do to solve a problem or situation and relate it to how you can use it to become an asset to the company.

Some traits that employers usually look for in a future employee are independence, dependability, flexibility, and confidence. These traits are crucial for any organization because it makes a good leader. Multitaskers are also vital to any company because they do what is necessary and not just stick to what they are used to. Use these skills to sell yourself and make sure to play the part.

One of the most important traits an employer wants to see from a candidate, it's hardworking. Provide proof statements of this positive trait, for instance, if you work late nights at the office and if you are the first to arrive in the morning and the last to leave at night. These statements will give employers a glimpse of your dedication to your job. Lastly, listen to your interviewer. You must not come across as someone who do know to listen and just speaks whenever he/she wants

TYPE OF QUESTIONS TO ASK AN INTERVIEWER

When you go through a job interview, you will be given the chance to ask questions for your employers to answers. These questions not only help you find out whatever it is that confuses you about the job or satisfy your curiosities about the job, asking the right questions also gives the interviewers and employers an impression of how much you want the job. This opportunity to ask questions usually happens at the end of the job interview. Preparing questions gives the employers the impression that you work hard to get what you want.

The best questions to ask an interviewer are usually open-ended ones because they create information-rich responses. The beauty of asking open-ended questions is that, these questions do not just answer yes or no. The responses are expanded and make you think well about the job you are applying for.

Employers learn a lot from the applicant not just through their answers to the questions they provide, but also through the things they want to know or how they collect and process these information. For employers, if an applicant does not ask questions regarding the job, they often wonder if they will ask questions when they get hired, and not asking questions also give a negative impression because it may often mean that you are being too confident about yourself and will not let anyone help you. In any job, being a team player is very important.

Some of the questions to ask at the end of an interview should include about the job position you are applying for. Here are some examples of questions:

- What are some of the daily duties and responsibilities this job requires?

- What are your expectations for this position?

- What are the challenges or struggles the company is currently facing?

- After this interview, what should I look forward to next?

- What is the best thing about working in this company?

- What are the top priorities this job position needs to accomplish?

- Do you have concerns regarding my ability to perform the job?

Furthermore, do not ask questions that are not thoughtful enough such as involving vacation leaves, benefits, absenteeism records, etc. Because employers consider these as dumb questions that will hurt your chances of getting the job you are applying for.

MISTAKES TO AVOID DURING A JOB INTERVIEW

During a job interview, not only do your answers are being analyzed, but also how you appear before the interviewer. To be able to get the job you desire, there are certain mistakes that you need to avoid and this chapter will give you some ideas of the things you shouldn't do when you come in for a job interview.

1. Dressing Unprofessionally.

Looks aren't everything, but when you are applying for a job, you should be able to look like a professional. Although attires vary depending on the job you are applying for, dressing up too casual or too revealing for the job interview doesn't give you an upper hand, thus it would only make you appear that you are not taking the job seriously.

2. Being Late for The Interview.

First impressions last. If you come in late for the interview, it would mean that you have an incredibly poor time management skills, which is one-trait employers absolutely dislike. This attitude suggests lack of respect for the company and interviewer. It is best to arrive around 10-15 minutes early for the job interview.

3. Using Your Phone During the Interview.

Talking about respect, one of the most disrespectful things to do during an interview is using your phone or checking your phone over and over again. This gives the interviewer a glimpse of a negative attitude you have.

4. Coming Unprepared.

Not knowing anything about the company and the job position during the interview is a big mistake to avoid because it means you did not do your homework, which gives the interviewer the impression that you are lazy.

5. Negative Body Cues.

Body language can make or break you. Not smiling and not making eye contact are some of negative body cues that interviewers consider while making the selection process. If you did these things, it will hurt your chances.

6. Bringing Food or Drinks During an Interview.

Yes, it is understandable that waiting will make you hungry or thirsty, but eating and drinking while the interview is ongoing is a big no. You can do it after the job interview.

7. Talking Too Much.

Job interviews require you to talk and sell yourself, but it doesn't mean that you have the liberty to talk about yourself for as long as you want. Remember that coming off as overconfident is also a negative trait for employers.

8. Criticizing Previous Employers.

There's such a thing as constructive criticism, but if criticizing past companies you work for just for the sake of proving a point is also a negative trait that must be avoided in an interview.

9. Not Doing Follow-Ups.

Applicants are to just leaving after the interview and expecting a call from the employer, but failing to follow-up on your application is also one mistake to avoid.

10. Being All About The Money.

Appearing that you are just after the money is a big mistake. Show off your skills and knowledge, but it is wrong to appear greedy during the interview.

IMPROVING YOUR CHANCES OF GETTING A JOB

Getting a job is not easy. It takes perseverance and a whole lot of patience to get through with the painstaking application process and a series of job interviews. Although it is hard to predict whether you have a shot at landing a job, there are also ways you can do to improve your chances of getting one. And although it seems that to it's easy for some people to find a job, trust me, they also do their part.

One way of improving your chances of getting a job is to not to be too picky when it comes to actually looking for one. You can never find a perfect job. There will always be parts of it that will tick you or you will probably regret doing, but at the end of the day, your job pays the bills. As long as you are working with integrity and the job doesn't require you to do things that are far too out of your job description, then it's okay. You can find better opportunities in the future.

Another way of improving your chances of getting a job is, well, to continue searching for job vacancies. If you happened to have a bad experience in the past regarding job applications, do not let that discourage you and just keep on looking for possible jobs you can apply for.

Preparation is key. Success happens to people who prepare and equip themselves with the right attitude and important skills. Focus on making an impressive resume, something the employers wouldn't pass up or ignore. More importantly, do not forget to make your cover letter a good one. Remember that cover letters might make or break your chances of landing that job interview.

It is important to have an extensive network. People who have a lot of connections often get better results. One way of networking is to attend different events or social gatherings. These days, it's actually easier because of the existence of social media such as Facebook, Twitter, LinkedIn, etc. Use these to expand your network. These people could help you find a job or even the job of your dreams.

Finally, one of the ways to improve chances of getting a job is to work on improving yourself and not ignoring jobs that are part-time or temporary. The knowledge and skills your will acquire from these jobs will help you a lot in getting a job because employers value experiences that would eventually help you become the best version of yourself and of course, a better employee.

TIPS ON HOW TO WORK WELL UNDER PRESSURE

Getting a job is only the beginning of a long journey of reaching the top. During job interviews, employers often ask how well a candidate works under pressure because it's one trait one must have in the corporate world, especially when being under pressure is almost a daily event. This chapter will hopefully provide some tips not to crack under pressure.

Look at pressure as a challenge. Working under pressure is something that you will encounter in the corporate world. It would definitely test your patience and your ability to cope and function during a time when you have to present to a group of bosses or very important people. One way to work well under pressure is to look at the situation as a challenge and not as a death sentence. The more you remind yourself that you will make mistakes or will mess up, the more it paralyzes you. Looking at it as an opportunity to do your job and provide help to others would give you more energy to do it well.

Try to assess and evaluate the situation first and foremost. Don't assume anything, and instead, assess the situation you are in and the problems you are facing. Most of the time, the worst scenarios you create inside your head end up not happening at all. Take a deep breath, and list down your plan of action. It would also help if you plan for the worst cases, not to make you even more anxious, but to allow you to prepare. Preparation ignites confidence because there's an assurance that you are taking your job seriously.

Take good care of yourself. One easy way to cope with stress that comes with being under pressure is to take care of yourself by getting enough sleep and eating the right kind food. Stressful jobs will wear you out so the most effective way to battle stress, anxiety, that will also help you deal better with pressure. Taking vitamins and eating nutritious foods to help you think well and perform better at work.

Listen to some music. Although not all jobs would permit you to do this, another way to work well under pressure is to listen to relaxing music. Music will help you calm down and decrease your level of anxiety. This would also distract you from whatever negative feelings you have at the moment, so instead of panicking, get your iPod and listen to relaxing sounds for a moment.

Ask for help. It is not wrong to ask some help from a co-worker or a friend you trust; so another way to function well under pressure is to tell someone about what you are going through and let him or her help you. Being a team player is not about taking it all in and solving problems on your own. The good thing about it is that it allows you to have people by your side to assist you and guide you when you are having a hard time. No man is an island.

GOOD HABITS OF SUCCESSFUL PEOPLE

Success doesn't come right away. You need patience, dedication, and the correct habits to reach the top. A lot of successful people share certain habits that led them to become very successful. This chapter lists down some of these habits that would hopefully give encouragement to you and would fuel you to start doing.

Reading is a powerful habit that successful people started doing at a young age. Never stop reading a variety of books because it helps you collect great information from different people with expertise on a variety of fields or careers. It was known that J.K. Rowling reads just about anything, and because of this habit, the rest is history. Reading helps you think outside the box and inspire you to do things that will benefit you and a lot of people. It is also important to highlight the things that you gather from reading and apply whatever you learned from it.

Another good habit that successful people share is waking up early. Waking up early is not easy because who doesn't love sleep? But early risers tend to make good use of their time, and it is no mystery that hard workers become someone people aspire to be because they get the results they have always wanted to get. So stop hitting the snooze button and get up early.

They listen to criticisms and never give up. Yes, at times criticisms will hurt your feelings, but you should not let these to get in the way of striving for your dreams. Successful people never gave up even after going through a lot of disappointments and failures. They kept standing up and figuring out their mistakes, and at the same time, they kept learning from it. Those obstacles will only make you wiser and tougher.

They don't always complain. Successful people also feel tired and irritated, but they are not big complainers or whiners. Complaining is such a waste of time and energy, so instead of whining when things don't go as they plan, they use their time to find solutions for their problems and do not allow themselves to be unproductive for long periods of time. They don't point fingers to other people when something fails. They either fix it right away or take their time to analyze the situation.

Lastly, successful people are perfectionists. They don't just settle for anything that is "good enough"; they want to be amazed by their work. They are ambitious and want to do something that has never been done before. They are innovators and they make it a point that these innovations will change the course of destiny, but at the same time, they set realistic goals. They know what they are passionate about and that makes it easier for them to do something about it.

HOW TO AVOID THE USE OF FILLERS

Did you know that fillers or filler words could hurt your chances of landing that dream job? Yes, it could. Almost every human being utter these words during speeches or interviews, but this shouldn't be the case. Some employers have zero tolerance for people who use these during an interview, and I know that they are very hard to stop using. Now the question is, is there a way for you to stop using fillers such us "um", "uh", "like", and "ah"? Of course there is.

This chapter will give tips on how to reduce them.

One way to help you reduce the use of fillers is to figure out how often you use them. Find someone who can be your audience that would help you count the number of times you use fillers during a speech or whenever you practice for your job interview. You can also use a recorder to record your voice and also yourself when you talk. When you are aware how often you use fillers, you'd be more conscious the next time you talk to an interviewer or an audience.

Fillers are often associated with anxiety or nervousness, but other studies show that we use fillers depending on our emotional state. For instance, did you notice that you don't usually use fillers when you talk to a close friend or a family member? Fillers are also indication that you are not done talking during a more formal conversation. They are sort of placeholders.

Another way of minimizing the use of fillers is preparation. Let's say you have an interview in a few days or a speech, prepare for the things you are going to say. Memorization by heart can also help eliminate the use of fillers. When you are confident about what you are going to say, you tend to not use fillers.

Another way to minimize the use of fillers is to keep your sentence straight to the point. When you use much simpler words and use them in shorter sentences, you end up not falling into the filler trap. Slowing down your speech can help you not use fillers as well. When you slow down, your brain is more able to keep up the pace. When you talk slower, the people who listens to you would be able to understand you better. Your words are more affective when you are understood well.

HOW TO LOOK CONFIDENT

Confidence is more than just acting like one; it's about actually feeling it. But just in case you are not as confident as you would like, there are ways you can make it look like you are self-assured and not dying inside.

This chapter is all about giving tips on how to appear confident before an interviewer or employer.

Confidence can be seen through your body posture. In order to appear confident, you must stop slouching. Sit up straight when you are waiting for you turn or stand tall when you enter an interview room or office. Bad postures usually make you appear like you don't know what you're into, and employers absolutely dislike it when they talk to someone who look like they don't want to be where they are. In order to look more confident, develop a good stance.

Another way to look confident is smiling. Smiling is an instant pick-me-upper, and it's the best accessory you will ever wear. When you smile, you appear more confident before another individual or a group of individuals. It also makes you look friendlier, which of course, is a great thing. You don't need to smile all the time, but people who don't smile enough end up looking more arrogant. First impressions last.

Practice eye-to-eye contact. When you look people in the eye, you instantly look confident. You don't need to look at them in the eye at all times because that will only make you look creepy, but when you talk to an employer, eye-to-eye contact is a must because it constitutes connection and respect.

Lastly, dress up well. A person is 100% more confident when they look and smell great. In order to impress at a job interview, you need to take care of your hygiene. If you are unsure of how you look, your confidence drops. Appearance is a powerful tool in making a good first impression. You should also practice having a positive and confident mindset. When your minds think that you are confident, your confidence shows on the outside as well.

WHAT TO WEAR TO AN INTERVIEW

Appearance is a powerful tool to get the job you are applying for. If you spend a lot of time preparing for your interview job questions, taking an extra time choosing what you will wear for your job interview is just as important. In a job interview, you are selling yourself to the employer, so you have to present yourself as someone who not only can do the job well, but someone who will be a great asset to the company.

This chapter will give you tips on what to wear during that job interview you will go to.

First and foremost, although not a lot of applicants do this but it is ok to ask what you should wear for your interview. You must be able to buy clothes that will make you look smart. For males, suits are the way to go. Solid blue or gray suits are preferable with shirt and a tie. You should also choose the right hairstyle for your job interview. There is such a thing as businessman's haircut, which appears to be short and well styled. You might also want to shave your facial hair before coming in for your interview because a clean shaven look usually means you are very serious about the job you are applying for. Take time to polish your shoe because dirty, unpolished shoes don't mean well to employers. It also means that you are not that interested in the job.

For females, black slacks are very essential because they go with almost anything. Invest in a pair of black slacks that you can use many times. Button down blouses are also popular for a lot of women. You can experiment with them, and they definitely look good in anyone. Just keep in mind that you should maintain that classy, modest look during a job interview. You can also invest in a navy blue blazer that fits well. You may also wear a dress and skirt for your interview. You should also wear heels because they help you look taller and more confident.

Colors have meanings. Out of all the colors you can wear, blue and gray are possibly the safest ones. According to some studies, the shades of blue exude credibility as well as trust. Employers also chose the color blue as a color they recommend applicants to wear during a job interview. Blue also exudes confidence, while gray exudes traits like being logical and analytical.

If there's a color you should probably avoid wearing, then it's brown. Brown actually makes you look old-fashioned, and that's not what you want to happen during your first meeting with your future employer. They don't have negative meanings or whatsoever, but they tend to appear boring.

CAREER MARKETING

Career marketing is essentially all about positioning yourself on the job market; to be able to think like an entrepreneur and how you would be able to find people that will appreciate what you are selling. Job seekers who don't plan to beforehand will eventually fail to enhance their job search, so it is very important to do your own career-marketing plan.

This chapter will give you tips on how to do career marketing and will enlighten you what it truly means for someone looking for a job.

The first thing you should know is that, in making your career marketing plan you should know what exactly you are looking for. Search for available jobs online that you would be interested in or the careers you'd be more than interested to pursue. When looking for careers related to your field, you should be aware of the current trends. To be able to do this, you need to do a lot of market researches.

The next thing you should understand about career marketing is you need to list down all the companies you are interested in applying to. If you are eyeing on specific companies, you need to research about them and gather enough information. You wouldn't be able to find success in just trying your luck and not knowing anything about potential employers especially in a very competitive industry. Focusing on the career you want to pursue and the companies you are interested in would help you set specific and realistic goals for yourself. When there's too much going on in your head, you wouldn't be able to concentrate.

In career marketing, you need to identify your strengths and weaknesses. For this, you can use the SWOT Analysis. This is a method used by many in figuring out the strengths, weaknesses, opportunities, and threats in a certain project or plan. This analysis is structured, so you would be able to plan carefully and by the end of this method, you have more solid plans for your growth as well as your plans for your career.

Lastly, career marketing involves you and knowing what makes you unique both as an individual and as an employee. Think of yourself as a product. What do you have that will make you stand out from the rest? What specific skills or abilities do you have that would impress others? Why should people patronize you? These are some questions that you need to ask yourself and hopefully figure out. When you do, list these all down. You need to position yourself properly in the job market so employers would be able to notice you. At the same time, work on your communication skills. In order to sell yourself, you must have exemplary communication skills. Some people are able to attract attention when they are able to impress others with the way they communicate.

TIPS TO OVERCOME EMPLOYMENT CHALLENGES

Disabilities could affect anyone's chances of getting the job they want, but that doesn't mean it should always be the case. There are ways you can minimize these effects so you would be able to function well in your workplace during an interview and when you finally get the job. The good thing is that, many countries have legal protection to those with people with disabilities so discrimination is against the law. However, it is important to prove yourself to your superiors, and this chapter hopefully gives you some ideas on how to manage employment challenges in the workplace.

More than anyone else, you know yourself. So you should be able to identify the skills you have that would make you stand out from other applicants. List down all your previous jobs and the skills you have acquired from them. Before you enter a workplace, make sure you have proof of your disability and the doctor's advice on the kinds of activities you will have a hard time doing. You should also identify all your physical abilities and how they will affect your job positively. Your mental skills are very important too. Your employer will evaluate how well you respond to your superiors and co-workers, as well as how much you understand a situation, a task and how able you are in providing solutions for it.

Take note of how you cope with changes in your environment, and let your interviewer and employer know about this. You should be able to identify situations that will have a negative effect on you such as temperatures and environment.

Look for jobs posted that specifically cater to people with disability. This would be very helpful for you to overcome challenges finding the job that would understand your limitations.

A lot of jobs posted on these sites provide services for specific issues. Hardworking and talented people with disabilities will never run out of opportunities when they know where to look at. If let's say, you haven't worked for a long time, there are a lot of job opportunities for you especially nowadays. Online job search makes it easier for people to find a job. Although it can only do so much, it is one step in getting that job in the corporate world. Think about all your achievement in the past and remind yourself of the things you can do to become an asset to a company.

Another way to minimize the effects of your disability to your job is to not dwell too much on whatever it is that you are going through and get your head on straight and set goals for yourself. When people see how much you want something regardless of your disability. Positive attitude reflects on the things you are doing, and at the same time it boosts your self-confidence.

COVER LETTER TIPS

Cover letters are just as important as resumes. If you think nobody reads them, then I have to tell you, they do. A good resume with a bad cover letter could hurt your chances of getting the job you are applying for. Some employers even consider them more important than resumes because they are able to tell them who's behind that resume, and although your resume would be able to tell a lot about how good you are as a student or a former employee, your cover letter will reveal some of most important traits hiring managers or employers look for in an applicant.

This chapter will hopefully help you accomplish that cover letter and impress hiring managers.

In making your cover letter, you need to understand that you don't need to repeat the information you have in your resume, instead, your cover letter should have details that you couldn't fit in your resume such as how you have handled problems in the past and how you were able to solve them. Give them reasons why you deserve the position by telling them how you applied skills in your personal and professional life. It's also very important that you know who you're writing to so take time finding out the hiring manager or employer's name.

Your cover letter should also let the employers know what you would be able to do for the company and why you are capable to do all the things the job requires. Employers also want to see in your cover letter not the skills you don't have, but those that you do. Highlight these as well as the experiences that were able to bring out the best in you. You may also add great feedback from your previous bosses and colleagues.

You should be able to show some personality in your cover letter. Being too formal doesn't count as showing personality. Show them an approachable, friendly persona-- someone who's great to have around. Try to sound a little bit excited in the cover letter and not too stiff, but still maintain that normal individual. When hiring managers see how much you want this job, they will give you a chance to present yourself.

Lastly, for you to be able to work on your cover letter easily, get inspiration from premade cover letters, but keep it as honest and as sincere as you can. Genuine writing goes a long way. Hiring managers like applicants that are not too concerned about the salary and more on the experience to be part of the company and contribute to its growth. Avoid sounding conceited on the page, like you are just bragging about your skills and abilities. Make sure to check your grammar and spellings before sending your cover letter.

CREATING A WINNING RESUME

Having a great resume is your ticket to landing the job of your dreams. In order to get that job, you must get a job interview first. And how do you get a job interview? You must first have an impressive resume. A resume has all the details regarding your name, where you went to college, the previous companies you worked for, achievements, etc. It also has some of your strengths and abilities.

This chapter is all about giving you 10 tips on how you can create an impressive resume.

1. Avoid long resumes. When your resume has too many details, you make the risk of boring hiring managers to death. Include the most important information on the first page of your resume. The most ideal

resume should only have one or two pages.

2. Never forget that basic information such as your name and contact details should be big enough to stand out from the rest of details on your resume. Your name should have the biggest font and contact details should be clear enough to understand.

3. Consider using bullet points. Instead of using long paragraphs that a lot of hiring managers have no patience to read, use bullet points to highlight important information about you such as your educational background and past work experiences.

4. Research on good summary statements that you can use to write your qualifications summary.

5. Avoid including long lists of the responsibilities you had during your

previous job. Instead, describe your professional achievements.

6. Use attention-grabbing titles. When you list down your previous work experiences, employers should already have an idea of the nature of those jobs.

7. If you have been working for more than 10 years, you don't need to put your older work experiences anymore because they would only take up a lot of space.

8. Always use action verbs such as solved, planned, accomplished, and achieved.

9. Don't include unnecessary information such as your hobbies, religion or beliefs, and anything that talks about your political stance or affiliation.

10. Your skills relevant to the job should be highlighted on your resume.

JOB INTERVIEW QUESTIONS & ANSWERS

If you really want to get that job you are interested in, the most important thing you should do is to ace your job interview. Interviewers from every company ask almost the same questions, but of course, how you answer these questions will land you that coveted job. This chapter will give you the 20 most common job interview questions and the ideas on how to answer these questions.

1. Tell me something about yourself. Now, this question is for you to make yourself feel comfortable. It is a way to break the ice. To answer this question, you can be creative by answering with personal interests or hobbies that don't have anything to do with the job.

2. What is your greatest strength? Your answer should be about the skills you have that the job

could definitely use. The skills that are required for this job should match those with your answers. You can brag a little bit, but remember to not overdo it.

3. Where do you see yourself in 5 years? Your answer should be about how your skills and contributions will have impacted the company in a good way by then. Do not focus on your aspirations, but more on the company you want to work for.

4. How do you handle pressure? Your answer should specifically about a stressful event or situation you were able to handle well. This would give the interviewer an idea how you were able to perform even under stressful circumstances.

5. How did you know about the position? If you heard about the position through a friend, its better you name-drop the person. If you found

it on a random website, mention how it caught your attention.

6. Why should we hire you? The best way to answer this is to both sell yourself and tell them the important things you know about the company. You should also emphasize your experiences as an employee and the skills that will make you stand out from the rest.

7. Why do you want this job? You should answer this by letting them know that you know that you can give great results and how your colleagues and the company will benefit from your contributions.

8. Why did you choose your course? Your answer should depend on how close the job you are applying for to your chosen major. You should be able to make connections to sell your answer to the employer.

9. What's your biggest achievement? Answer this by telling a show story on how you were able to accomplish a great result as an employee.

10. What's your dream job? The best way to answer this is to tell them your true aspirations, but keep in mind that the employer also wants to make sure whether you are the perfect fit for the job, so it's better your response will lean towards the field you are interested in.

11. Do you have any pending applications? The best way to answer this is to say that you are currently applying to several other companies or firms that will let you apply your abilities or skills.

12. What kind of work environment do you prefer? Your answer should be similar to the company's work environment you are applying to.

13. How would your colleagues describe you? You have to be as honest as possible when you answer this. At the same time, this could be an opportunity for you to elaborate more on your strengths.

14. How would you describe yourself? Answer truthfully and at the same time, try to make connections to the job requires.

15. What are you salary requirements? It's not wrong to be honest, but you should have an idea about how the position you're applying for really get paid.

16. What do you do if you're not working? Try to sound fun but not someone who gets drunk all the time.

17. What is your greatest weakness? You can be truthful about answering this and really think about what you need help on, but try to make it

sound something not too bad or something you can improve with the help of your team.

18. Why do you want to quit your job? Respond with something about how much you want to explore other opportunities, but do not bad mouth your previous employers.

19. What were your responsibilities? Respond with detailed summary of your responsibilities from your previous or current job that will match the responsibilities of the job you are applying for.

20. Do you have any questions for us? Respond with a couple of smart questions your interviewer can answer.

JOB INTERVIEW BODY LANGUAGE

Body languages speak louder than words especially during job interviews. Your job interview doesn't start and end in question and answer. Keep in mind that interviewers or hiring managers are trained to read body language. This chapter will give you ideas about effective body languages you should use during your job interview.

1. Stand straight or rest your back against the chair. Slouching means lack of confidence. Project confidence as soon as you walk in that door.

2. Use hand gestures while speaking. Don't hide your hands if you're unsure of what

to do. Go ahead and use hand gestures while talking.

3. Nod while listening. Nodding means you are paying attention to what they're saying as well as enjoying your time.

4. Leaning in while having a conversation with an employer or interviewer means being interested.

5. Shake hands using your right hand and try not to be too aggressive. Offering your hand showing your palms usually means respect.

6. Maintain eye-to-eye contact but not too intensely. Too direct would creep your interviewer out. Refrain from looking down.

7. Smile when appropriate. Smiling creates a friendly atmosphere.

BEST WAYS TO NETWORK

There is no secret to effective networking. It is something that can be developed and learned. Networking is also a tool to sell yourself to different employers and companies, and at the same time expand your professional network.

This chapter will give you ideas on the best ways to network for your professional career.

1. Do your homework. It is important to actually know what you are saying. Confidence follows when you are well prepared because you'd be able to answer questions headed your way. You should always prepare questions to ask.

2. Provide Business Cards. Business Cards are necessary to exchange contact numbers and details. Make sure that you have plenty so you won't need to worry about running out of them, especially during meetings with important people.

3. Do Listen. Listening is an important part of networking. You are not making conversations just for one goal, but you also need to listen and learn from other people you meet.

4. Be Patient. Developing relationships takes time. People who are impatient tend to ruin business deals and relationships.

5. Do not limit yourself to one person. Speak to plenty of people. Making connections is very important for effective networking. Engage in different activities that you have always been interested to try. If it's possible, reconnect with your contacts from before.

6. Create a Twitter or a Facebook Account. These days, social networking is a powerful tool in bridging a gap or creating channels.

7. Maintain a friendly image. Who wants to talk to someone who comes across as arrogant? Keep in mind to always look your best and be confident. You don't know whom you'll run into during events.

8. Entertain people. Be entertaining without coming across as trying too hard. Show personality and be respectful at the same time.

9. Do volunteer work. There are a lot of nonprofit organizations you could go to and from there, you'd be able to meet people who are influential. Take this opportunity to get to know professionals.

10. Meet your online contacts. Use social media platforms to expand your network.

TIPS FROM THE BOSS

Let's get real for a minute. Shall we?

I've ran over 10 businesses in the last 19 years and have been an employee for about 8 years. There's a very different mentality that both sides take.

As an employee it's easy to feel entitled. We want to know how much money we are going to make. We want to know how much we're going to have to do. We want to know what benefits we receive. There's a lot of wants. We also, at least some of the time want to do the least possible work without getting fired. Seen the movie "Office Space"?

If not I truly recommend it.

This is not just entitlement. Its reality. If I know that no matter how hard I work I will still make the same amount where is the motivation?

Are we on the same page?

I thought so.

Let's switch perspectives.

Most of company owners start out of necessity. Sure, we are inspired and a few of us have rich families and get funded… but that's not the majority. The media always shows the extreme examples to make us feel as if we aren't good enough.

Most of us start with little money and bootstrap the business.

Most of us do not pay ourselves a salary for a long time and live in horrible conditions.

Most of us don't have any benefits and nobody to help us when things go wrong.

Eventually we learn that we cannot do it all by ourselves and we start hiring.

Then we often get the type of person I mentioned in the beginning. Unless you are joining a huge corporation… there's no room for error. Small businesses die a quick death.

The bottom line for an employer is the actual value that you bring to the business. That means… does this person justify me paying them?

Here's an example:

You are paid to answer calls and make sales.

I pay you a $100 per day. You think to yourself that it's not enough because you're working all day and make a lot of sales.

In reality you make 3 sales per day on average.

The product/service costs the customer $200 each. It costs my company a $170 to fulfill that order before paying you.

That leaves me with $90 per day. Not enough to pay you and am not making anything for myself. Simply said... you're not worth it to me unless you can make an additional sale.

Want a raise?

Forget about it. I already lose money with you around.

This works in all careers whether its sales or services.

The problem that we often encounter is that the owner themselves don't actually know exactly how much you are worth. Then all logic goes out the window and everybody stays confused. That is not a healthy environment.

WHO GETS PROMOTED?

This is simple.

We work with people we like.

We work with people others respect.

We work with people who take care of themselves and others.

We work with people that create more value than they take.

If you're at a company where your value is not clearly defined... then you have to try and figure this out for yourself or better yet... switch to a smarter ran company. I often recommend starting a business, even if it is a hobby or something small on the side to figure out the realities and see if you have what it takes to do so successfully. It might be that you are simply not meant to be an employee and getting promoted is not the best thing for you. On the other hand, you might quickly realize that running a business comes with so many problems and headaches that it is better to simply be an employee. At the end of the day, it is very important to make that decision yourself and not feel like a victim. Nobody is happy in such a situation.

I'm happy Anne Johnson allowed me to add a few things to this book.

If you'd like to hear more from me or contact me go to smartbrandmarketing.com

I also filmed a movie showing the realities of successful business owners who do so while traveling the world. You can find it at yourownwayout.com

Good luck to you!

TL

Made in the USA
Charleston, SC
03 November 2016